SUMMARY

THE PLANT PARADOX

THE HIDDEN DANGERS IN "HEALTHY" FOODS THAT CAUSE DISEASE AND WEIGHT GAIN

By
Steven R. Gundry M.D.

**Proudly Brought to you by
OneHour Reads**

Table of Contents

EXECUTIVE SUMMARY

In "The Plant Paradox: the hidden dangers in 'healthy foods' that cause disease and weight gain", Dr. Steven Gundry sets out to demystify long-held myths about plant-based foods. These foods, believed for the most part, to be healthy, have been responsible for hurting the human body for so long.

Gundry exposes the real cause of weight problems, and if you're one of those people who seem to be eating right and doing all the right exercises, yet suffering weight problems and related diseases, then you'll want to read this book. Gundry's book contends that your weight loss efforts are failing not because of any fault of yours, but because you're mostly misinformed.

He begins with a detailed description of the problem and how it came to be; problematic foods and how they interact with our body system to cause us harm. This is followed by instructions on how to undo the damage that has been done, and finally, how to rid yourself of illnesses and diseases by eating the right foods.

PART I: THE DIETRY DILEMA

CHAPTER 1: THE WAR BETWEEN PLANTS AND ANIMALS

Key Takeaways:

- *Vegetables and fruits are not always our friend*
- *Whole-grain foods are not the healthy choice as we've been told*
- *Plants try to survive by producing noxious chemicals to dissuade predators from eating them*
- *Lectins are protein substances produced by plants, and they disrupt cell functioning in predators, including humans. This malfunction results in sicknesses and diseases, and more commonly, gut problems.*

As you begin reading this book, be prepared to go on a fact-finding journey. Apart from the fact that it's a journey that will help you become healthier, you will get to understand plants and exactly how they work. For so long, we have remained ignorant about the plants- grains, fruits, veggies, etc. - that we eat. They are more than items on our menu. Like every other living thing, they are designed with defensive mechanisms- devices put in place to keep their kind from extinction. Some of these protective devices include toxins and as humans, we fall into the category of 'enemies' from whom these plants require protection.

Plants are also the most nutritious meals any human can have, hence, the allusion to irony in the title of this book.

The plant paradox program advocated in this book has been successful in producing significant results with weight problems, both healthy weight loss and healthy weight gain. Yes, it contains the right kind of plants, specific varieties of fish as well as grass-fed meat.

Probably the first of the seemingly weird stuff you'll hear on this journey is this: folks who ate less fruit, more egg yolks, and less seedy veggies experienced a marked improvement in their overall health. The predicament on which this book is premised lies in a feature that all living things possess: survival instinct. Just as humans have that innate drive for preservation, so do the plants that end up on our dinner plates. And just as we have survival techniques against our enemies, plants do as well, and yes, you guessed it, we are one of their enemies because we eat them. In this way, the plant kingdom has always been in contention with the animal kingdom.

There are plants and there are plants. While we've been told for so long that vegetables and fruits are our friends, you might actually want to be careful on that. Some plant constituents, such as Gluten, do more harm than good to the body. But despite all the fuss about Gluten, they're only one kind of lectins, a protein that is extensively discussed in this plant irony. This book presents a more thorough perspective on the peculiarities of plants and how these so-called good foods sometimes cause us to add unhealthy weight and develop chronic illnesses. Far from it, this is not about dissuading you from eating plants and vegetables. On the contrary, this is about eating the right plants, and eating them the right way.

In the Prey-Predator dynamic, it would appear the scales are naturally tipped in favor of animals; they can walk, run, or fly from enemies seeking their lives. Unlike plants, you say? Well, even though plants cannot move, they have developed other methods of protecting themselves from enemy attack. When they first emerged on earth approximately 450 million years ago, it was smooth sailing so to speak. There were no animals to threaten their existence and no particular need for protection. When animals showed up some 90 million years later, it stopped being business as usual. Their new neighbors found plants desirable and did not mind helping themselves to some. The immovable creatures became at risk of extinction, so they devised various means of staying alive. Some of those means have to do with physical properties- evolving harder exteriors; developing color to blend with the environment to prevent detection, etc. Another means, which is of great significance to us, was the production of substances deadly to their predators. They locate them in strategic places, like the seed, that life-carrying plant part.

Plants are good at fighting with chemical weapons, either to keep away predators by possibility of potential harm or make it difficult to digest their seeds, retaining their chances of survival. Interestingly, plants are even able to manipulate their animal predators into obeying orders.

Plants began to produce lectins when their first animal hunters- the insects- came to be. The lectins were capable of rendering any wandering insect incapacitated. Insects are not the same as humans, yes, but that doesn't mean the lectins poisonous to insects have no effect on the latter. There are obvious biological differences between a man and a grasshopper, but that only means that lectins have a subdued effect on the human system.

Instead of completely disabling a human being, lectins gradually hurt our system, resulting in a breakdown after many years. In some humans, certain lectins are immediately deadly, as with peanuts, but for the vast majority, we have no idea of the damage being done to our bodies as we consume what we think is healthy. Folks who possess immediate sensitivity to these specific lectins can be likened to methane and carbon-monoxide- sensitive canaries found most useful by coal miners.

If you never knew before, seeds are plant offspring that develop to become a new generation of plants. No thanks to the intense competition in nature, only a fraction of those produced eventually germinate into full-grown plants. Plants are aware of this unfortunate fact. Their seeds can be either of two types:

- The ones intended to be eaten by predators
- Those not meant to be eaten

Seeds within the first category are usually surrounded by tough protective material that keeps the seed on a journey through the predator's digestive system and out through excretion. This is actually the parent plant's strategy all along: life-bearing seed is transported by the hunter to another location to prevent the new life hustling for scarce resources in the same location as its parent. It also means the species is now more widespread.

Such seeds have no need to produce chemical defenses because their exterior is hard enough to serve as protection. Instead, they do all they can to get the predator to eat. For instance, such plants display a green color to signify an unripe state when their seed is yet to be covered completely. At this stage, they also produce harmful substances, just in case any predator (including you) fail to get the color message.

Similarly, they adopt a specific color to signify that they are ripe. In other words, their seeds- or offspring- have been fully coated in hard, protective material. It is at this point also that fructose, a kind of sugar produced by fruits, is highest. Fructose, unlike Glucose, does not trigger a feeling of fullness, which means predator gets to eat more seeds and the plant's chances of continued existence is increased.

Unfortunately, this phenomenon does not benefit us humans today. Our ancestors who were mostly hunters and gatherers may have thrived in spite of piling calories, but not us. Our lifestyles are way different and besides, they always ate fruit in season- once every year, in summertime- while we have technological advancements to thank for making fruit accessible to us every day of the year. Should we be surprised that obesity and chronic diseases have become the order of the day?

In most cases, the specific color adopted by plants to alert predators to their edible state is either orange, red, or yellow. For some reason, those colors confer the qualities of sugariness and attractiveness on the specific plant, drawing more and more predators in. This is the way of nature. Today, however, the trending practice is to pluck unripe fruits so they can survive transportation across long distances to where they'll be eventually sold. Getting there, they'll be forced to ripen by gassing with ethylene oxide. They look ripe, but naturally, they are not. In other words, they still contain a high amount of poisonous lectins. This is why fruits grown locally, and eaten in season, are the best for your health.

Now, seeds that fall within the second category do not have a tough casing. They don't need their offspring scattered abroad; these plants want their offspring taking over their spots so they don't need predators for any form of transportation. The goal here is to keep predators away and this they do by producing harmful chemical substances that are potent enough to debilitate the target. Some of those chemicals include:

- **LECTINS**- they interfere with cellular functioning by causing a couple of things, for instance, they are responsible for what you probably know as leaky gut.

- **PHYTATES-** anti-nutrients that make it impossible for the body to soak up important minerals
- **TRYPSIN INHIBITORS-** these make digestion a burden. They impede the processes of digestive enzymes and ultimately, predator's growth.
- **TANNINS-** they protect the plant by giving it a bitter taste that is obviously not appealing
- **ALKALOIDS-** commonly found in the stems and leaves of nightshades such as potatoes and peppers, they cause inflammation.

You know an interesting fact? The first three substances can all be found in your whole grains? Doesn't sound so healthy now, does it?

By now, you're probably wondering how plants manage to reason and how they weave such intricate plots to trick predators- including us- in a bid to elongate their existence. You'll be wrong to think that plants think just as humans do, but every living thing is programmed with the need to have their genes preserved. As such, any substance that makes this possible is good, as far as a plant is concerned. It would interest you to know that plants have awareness of when they're being eaten. No, it's not hearsay; it's scientifically proven. Studying the Thale Cress and the sensitive plant confirmed that plants go into defense mode and display distinct behaviors in the event that they're about to be eaten. They are also sensitive to changes in the day as they attach certain events to certain times.

Then of course there are Lectins; proteins produced by plants to defend themselves while harming us in the process. In fact, they are one of the major devices through which plants preserve themselves. Until 1884, the world had no idea that lectins existed and even at that point till this moment, the spotlight has been on Gluten, which is only one of the many lectins in existence and at work in our bodies.

Lectins can be situated in a number of places in a plant- leaves, seeds, skins, grains, etc. – and when they are consumed by predators, find carbohydrates or polysaccharides to attach themselves to. Their default location is the cell surface, where they can interfere with cell functioning of the said predator. As though this were not enough, lectins also assist bacteria and viruses in doing their dirty jobs, making their hosts more prone to such infections. And then of course there's the fact that they trigger weight gain, as evident in the functioning of Wheat Germ Agglutinin (WGA) present in wheat.

The actions of lectins can impair or completely destroy an animal predator. Either way, chances are that insects and other animals that have been hurt by certain plants will avoid such in future, giving the seeds of such plants a higher chance of survival. Our hunter-gatherer ancestors devised ingenious ways of coping with lectins, but not us. The most we do is create a drug to combat the effects and just go on eating the culprit. We make matters worse by making other animals- like the cows we feed on- eat these dangerous foods. Naturally, cows feed on grass, but no thanks to industrialization, we're more concerned with fattening these cows up at a faster rate so we feed them corn and soybeans. When they get heartburns just like humans do, we pump them full with chemical substances to relieve the symptom and make sure they continue eating food that is unhealthy for them, and us.

As humans, we are yet to develop full immunity against the onslaught of lectins found in plants- legumes, wheat, grains, etc. – but we consume them, and have an array of diseases, including gastric troubles, to show for it. And maybe if it was confined to plant foods, we wouldn't be in such a mess, but since we now feed our cows, poultry, and seafood with the same diet, we also consume lectins when we eat those animals and their products (egg, milk, meat, etc.). It would seem that now, we have no place to hide. Accept it or not, whenever you eat, you're not only eating that particular food item, but also everything that was fed to that food. Choosing to eat only organic plants and grass-fed animal products is not about being trendy; it's about choosing good health.

Before you start to think you're powerless against the effects of lectins, you should know that every animal has a developed defense strategy against lectins, and so do humans:

- The phlegm in your mouth and the nose mucus help to shut in lectins. These secretions contain a bunch of sugars, and we already know that's what lectins bind to. So your saliva and mucus prevent the lectins from making it all the way to the entire body.

- Your stomach acid is capable of digesting lectins, but only those of a certain kind.
- Certain bacteria reside in your mouth and gut. Their job is to neutralize the effects of plant lectins that you eat regularly. Because of the regularity in your consumption of such plants, the bacteria create in you a kind of immunity to the lectins.
- Mucus produced in the intestines provide a protective covering against the effects of lectins all over the body.

As powerful as these are, they can be weakened if you continue to eat more and more lectins. And the weaker they get, the closer lectins get to your gut cells. This is here your most valuable weapon comes in. You have a brain. You can avoid certain foods or disable the harmful effects of lectins by fixing the food in a certain way. Your defense structure is not unknown to the plants as well, and they come at you in 3 ways:

- Breaking through the intestinal lining
- Plants trick our defense system by making lectins to resemble certain useful proteins in our body.
- Lectins imitate real hormones and use that to carry out miscommunication among the cells. This results in sicknesses and diseases, as well as obesity.

Again, this is not to condemn all plants as evil. We *need* plants! We just need to know which plants to eat, when to eat them, in what quantity to eat them, and the best way to prepare them to reduce the effects of lectins.

CHAPTER 2: LECTINS ON THE LOOSE

Key Takeaways:

- *Lectins are unavoidable. You can only choose which you eat, and in what quantity.*
- *Predators are of two types: Grazers and Tree dwellers*
- *Commercial agriculture, altered cow milk, new world plants, & food processing introduced our bodies to strange lectins*
- *Gluten is not such a bad guy; WGA is*
- *By all means, avoid whole grain*
- *Lectins are responsible for virtually every health problem there is today*

Lectins have been around since forever, but not until recently did they begin to constitute such a life-threatening bunch. Our ancestors gained their first upper hand against lectins when they discovered fire. The heat of cooking helped to drastically reduce the power of lectins and disintegrate a plant's cell wall. It meant they used less energy for digestion and could afford more calories for their brain. It also meant humans could now eat tubers. Yams and potatoes have not always been a part of the human diet. Naturally, they constitute an integrated system by which plants store starch, and because of their size, were not considered edible by early humans.

With the advent of agriculture, legumes and grains became quite popular because of their cost effectiveness. Now, they appeared to be the key to human sustenance, but what we did not know was that they were going to introduce our bodies to never-before-seen lectins. Our bodies were not prepared.

Just as there are two kinds of seeds, there are also two kinds of predators, and both have different feeding patterns.

- **GRAZERS**- these are the animals that developed to feed on plants with one leaf, or as they are also called, monocotyledons. Cows and antelopes fall under this category.
- **TREE DWELLERS**- these animals evolved to feed on two-leaf plants, tree leaves, and fruit. Man belongs in this category.

As you might guess, one-leaf plants contain different kinds of lectins from the two-leaf plants. In this way, animals in each category have grown used to dealing with- absorbing and excreting- the kinds of lectins contained in their food. This also means they have been able to develop defense strategies, or immunity, against said lectins. So then, as humans, we have inherited gut bacteria that are capable of dealing with lectins peculiar to two-leaf plants.

These bacteria have been responsible for protecting our bodies from lectins; screening which lectins can or cannot go through. For thousands of years, they have developed into a predictable, effective system but no thanks to the new foods that made their way into our diets- bringing along with them new lectins- chaos has been the result. The new introductions have bombarded our bodies with substances that specialize in making our body go haywire.

Over the years, there have been four main occurrences; changes that have eroded the equilibrium existing between us humans and the plants that we consume. With each change, our guts have been coerced into dealing with unfamiliar lectins present in new food modifications, and with chronic illnesses at an all-time high, this doesn't look to be working out too well. These changes include:

- **Agricultural innovation and the popularity of legumes and grains.** The discovery and consequent cultivation of these foods meant more food was available for the exploding human population. But it also meant our immune structures were being forced to deal with strange lectins and because they had no prior knowledge of these lectins, they failed often. Ask the Egyptians who consumed a lot of grains back in the day. Diabetes, obesity, and heart-related diseases were a common occurrence thanks to the abundance of simple sugars they absorbed from their grain-heavy diet. In fact, oatmeal- a meal popularly conceived as healthy- has been linked severally to dental problems. Later on, humans would learn to mitigate these effects by inventing new ways of preparing legumes and grains.

- **Sudden alteration in cow milk.** Close to two millenniums ago, cows in Northern Europe suddenly began to produce an unhealthy variant of protein-casein A-1- instead of the usual casein A-2. This problematic protein is converted to lectins in the process of digestion, and this new lectin launches an assault on the immune system of people who eat it. Whether it's the meat, milk, or the cheese, casein A-1 is detrimental to human health. The situation is worse because farmers prefer such cows are more robust and produce far more milk than normal. If you can't get casein A-2 milk, then go with goat milk or sheep's.

- **Influx of new world plants and vegetables.** Until about five hundred years ago, most of the plants we eat today did not exist. Plants like squash, cashews, chia, and pumpkins were brought by explorers into the Americas. Yes, you guessed it, these new plants came along with a whole new set of lectins that our bodies- gut microbes, immune system- had no prior experience of.

- **Finally, food processing and innovations in commercial cultivation.** The food innovations we've witnessed in the last fifty years have contributed to the introduction of strange lectins. Food processing is the norm these days. We're always eating something out of a can or half-prepared; speedy meals we only need to pop into the microwave.

Genetic modification, antibiotics, agriculture chemicals, etc. are also some of these new changes that have plagued our bodies with lectins it knows nothing about fighting.

In evolution, the time within which our bodies are being introduced to these new lectins is extremely short. Our microbiomes are not adjusted to dealing with these strangers, and worse still, medications and chemicals continue to destroy these microbiomes, leaving the human body mostly defenseless.

There are many reasons for the fact that lectins are causing more damage for us than they did during any other time in history. For one, we have completely deviated from our forebears' way of eating and preparing food. Today, hardly does anybody cook; processed and semi-processed foods to the rescue! Don't forget that most of these foods also contain soy, corn, and wheat: poster foods for lectins. More than ever, our bodies are also having to deal with strange chemicals- antibiotics, fertilizers, preservatives, hand sanitizers, skincare products, etc. This onslaught of chemical substances continues to weaken our bodies and make it difficult for us to tolerate strange lectins.

Sadly, the line between healthy and unhealthy foods is very blurred, and when we eat the wrong things in the wrong proportions and prepared wrongly, all hell is let loose. Here lies the problem: many of us already think we're eating healthy even though our health is failing. Foods like beans, soy, sugar, flour, tofu, and potatoes have been believed long as healthy. In many programs however, restricting these foods have resulted in better health for patients. Significant changes such as disappearance of cancers have even been recorded.

Whether a food is lectin-rich or not, it has its good and bad sides, and besides, people can handle lectins at different levels. Our immune systems, gut layer, and the interaction of microbiome all function differently, so one person might be immune to lectins while another is highly allergic to it. The fact that a food is deemed healthy does not change the fact that it contains a lot of lectins. So, no matter how healthy you think a food is, you'll do well to stay away from it- or reduce your intake- if it contains a lot of lectins.

For so many years now, gluten has been demonized, and maybe that's not totally uncalled for. Gluten, after all, is a kind of lectin that contributes to celiac disease and a bunch of other unpleasant conditions. But Gluten is only one of the many lectins in existence and there are so many foods prominent in our diet that contain these other lectins. Unfortunately, virtually every grain contains lectins. Folks avoid foods containing gluten but are still eating those with other lectins, then they wonder why they're still piling on the pounds. Abstaining from anything gluten also means the gluten-eating microorganisms in your body starve and die away. This may not seem like a bad thing, until you eventually get to eat something containing gluten and your body revolts dangerously because it lacks the required microorganisms to absorb gluten.

Just as animals are plumped up with a diet of grains and antibiotics, so do humans. Maybe it's not exactly in the sense of animals, but think about it. Wheat is one of the most popular American food ingredients; we just seem to be hooked on wheat products. When we add that to our intake of antibiotic medications, the result is an increase in obesity and other weight-related diseases. Worse still, even when we're not consuming the wheat directly, we're doing it indirectly from the animals and animal products we eat.

Interestingly, gluten is not the thing to fear in wheat. A deadlier fellow is Wheat Germ Agglutinin (WGA), another lectin. WGA not only triggers weight accumulation, it is also culprit in diverse conditions such as inflammation, neural complications, diabetes, cell destruction, auto-immune diseases, kidney diseases, etc. You'll totally want to avoid any kind of whole-grain food, even though for so long they have been considered the healthy choice. Whole grain foods- cereal, bread or whatever- come packed with WGA and the effects of their popularity in the American society can be seen on our health. Unlike the French who relish their white bread without getting fat or falling victim to heart disease, our society is rife with these conditions.

In a bid to satisfy growing needs of the human population, commercial agriculture was born, and with it, chemical fertilizers, pesticides, and genetic mutations to make plants more resistant to pests. The last practice basically requires injecting more lectins into the plants to make them more undesirable to predators. So you see how we're eating more lectins than any of our ancestors ever did? Lectins are unavoidable but it's up to you to decide which ones you want to expose your body to, and in what amount. With most naturally occurring lectins, the amount consumed makes the entire difference. In reasonable quantities, lectins provide a sort of roadmap for the immune system.

Many of the crimes erroneously attributed to gluten are in fact due to other factors. One, most baked goods are now risen with transglutaminase, a yeast substitute that is detrimental to the body. Secondly, processed foods that include whole grains in their ingredient list usually require preservatives that are hazardous to human health. An example is Butyl HydroxyToluene (BHT).

The human immune system works like a sensor on the lookout for things that either help or hurt our bodies. When it recognizes the latter, it then sends out an SOS throughout the body, such that the unwanted organism has no chance against the various defenses located throughout the body. Lectins, on their part, specialize in pretending to be useful agents while upsetting the communication between cells and causing the body to turn against itself. This phenomenon is the sole cause for many of the illnesses we suffer today. It is also important to note that one person's immune system may react differently to lectins than the other. Factors such as genetics come into play in this dynamic.

CHAPTER 3: YOUR GUT UNDER ATTACK

Key Takeaways:

- *We need the holobiome to survive*
- *The gut microbes and humans are supposed to have a symbiotic relationship*
- *Your gut wall is supposed to keep strange things from getting into your bloodstream*
- *You inherited your mum's holobiome before you developed your own*
- *Autoimmune diseases are caused by issues in the gut*

The health issues you have are caused by very little things. Many microbes exist in parts of our bodies. Our biggest health myths spring up from the fact that we do not know that these microbes are a huge part of us. More so, close to 100% of our cells and genes are non-human. We and the microbes depend on each other for life and existence; we cannot do without them as they cannot without us. We house them on our skin and in our gastric tract and they in turn perform life functions to make sure we operate properly. The collection of these minute things is called microbiome or holobiome. It is difficult to admit but we need the microbiome to survive; our lives are hinged on them.

The microbes which are housed in the gastrointestinal (GI) tract absorb plant cells and convert it to energy in form of fat. We cannot do this of ourselves; we need the microbes to break it down for us. The functions of these microbes are to obtain energy from plants that have been consumed by the host and to guard the immune system of the host. Some scientists believe that we depend on the holobiome to act as a sentry for our immune system. There are various places where these microbes are located in and work in different animals; it is the stomach or multiple stomachs for cows and ruminants; the small intestine for the gorillas and other primates and the large intestine for man.

The GI tract (from your mouth to your anus) and all that is contained in your intestines is outside your body. Your food passes through you and when you eat food, it does not go "inside" you but it is outside you. Your intestinal wall separates the microbes in your gut from you. Your skin houses many skin microbes and it shields you from the outside world and to take in and excrete materials. The intestinal wall is somewhat similar to the skin inside out but the pressing function is to take in food. However, it is only one cell thick and stops strange material from penetrating your bloodstream and tissues. The goal is to keep the things contained in your intestine and the microbes where they belong: outside you so they do not cause trouble if they get inside.

Babies born through their mom's birth canals inherit their mom's microbe to make up their first holobiome. This holobiome initiates a baby's immune system and cells before the baby develops its own. In the last trimester of a mother's pregnancy, lactobacilli (microbes that live on lactose) moves to the mother's birth canal. Also, a mother's breastmilk has compound sugar fragments that the baby cannot break down; however it is essential of the development of the baby's microbes. A baby's immune system cannot mature properly without the microbes from the mother and if a baby was delivered through the cesarean section, the microbes and immune system of the baby would not develop fully till after six months.

There are many microbes in the holobiome which are housed in your body and constitute you. They are quite important because they perform tasks in the immune, nervous and hormonal systems and the organisms located in the GI tract are to break down food you cannot and convert it to energy for you and serve as a guard against toxic things you consume like lectins.

The non-human cells should function outside your body like on the skin and lining of the intestine and send nutrients to your body and not on the inside of the body. Though this is the ideal, it is a herculean task to keep the intestinal organisms where they belong because the intestinal wall is not thick enough to perfectly keep the microbes outside the gut and absorb nutrients.

It is food broken down into tiny particles by the microbes in your gut which is converted into energy or nutrients that should get into you. Your veins and lymph system is the portal through which this is done and it can only take little particles at a time. When the big molecules somehow get into your system, your immune system starts to ring warning bells. Because of the changes in diet and how foods are improved, these big particles such as lectins now get through the intestinal wall and then your immune system reacts. As your immune system tries to defend you, these lectins fuse such that your body cannot take in the nutrients it needs. Health practitioners do not know about the harm caused by lectins so they do not warn you against it. Non-steroidal anti-inflammatory drugs (NSAIDs) harm the lining of the small intestine which destroys the wall that keeps lectins and other harmful things from getting inside of you.

Bacteria located in layers of cells in the gut live on fructooligosaccharides, compound starches and they live in mucus. This mucus helps to block lectins from getting into you so mucus is beneficial. Using NSAIDs frequently is shooting yourself in the leg because it creates holes in your intestinal wall and gives access to foreign material. Your body starts to fight by causing pain and then you take in some more NSAIDs; and you keep going in circles. Increased penetrations by lectins, NSAIDs and other harmful materials lead to the leaky gut syndrome.

Auto-immune diseases are caused by penetration of your gut, intestinal wall and gut layer and can be healed by healing your gut. This penetration does not appear immediately but it damages your intestines to the extent that they cannot absorb nutrients anymore. The good news is that it can be repaired. Microbes help you to break down food but they are also guardians of your immune system. You and the microbes are inter-dependent. The friendly ones help you convert food to energy and protect you while you house them and feed them. However, the bad microbes are selfish and only meet their wants and needs so they make you crave for fast food, sugar and junk. The good microbes treat you right but the bad ones do not. You have to admit that these microbes exert a lot of influence over you.

The vagus nerve similarly known as the sympathetic nerve system is the longest nerve that connects the brain to the gut and so lectins can reach the brain through the vagus nerve. There are many neurons in your digestive system and if there is a second brain, it is in your gut and it is controlled by these microbes. You need the right microbes to enjoy good health and you can achieve this by feeding the good microbes what they need to survive and scrapping sugar foods that bad microbes thrive on. The interactions between you and your holobiome has been compromised as a result of prescription drugs, changes in diet and other factors but it is not the end of the road.

It is important we know about the Seven Deadly Disruptors so that we can eliminate them. They have been controlling what you consume and the health care products you use. They are very negligible and they give lectins access to your intestinal wall. To get back on a perfect health track, you need to stick to proper diet, key supplements and some everyday life changes.

CHAPTER 4: KNOW THY ENEMY-THE SEVEN DEADLY DISRUPTORS

Key Takeaways:

- *Quality of life should be your goal alongside longevity*
- *Antibiotics, Non-Steroidal Anti-inflammatory Drugs, Stomach Acid blockers, Artificial sweeteners, Endocrine disruptors, Genetically Modified Foods and exposure to blue light are things that have destroyed your gut flora*
- *All these things have friendly substitutes*

Altercations to our health are so gradual that we barely notice it until they become full blown. And when they become full blown, we want to eat more unhealthy foods or use drugs. Unfortunately, the drugs and medical procedures attempt to make us healthy but they do not. It appears like things are better because the life expectancy is longer as a result of more children immunization and reduced mortality rates but are we healthy? Many people "manage" most of their later years and we have prolonged people's sick lives with a host of medical procedures but that it is not living well. The number of years and quality of years must go hand in hand.

The things we consume everyday slowly cause paradigm shifts in the way we interact with our holobiome. Our new sources of food, food processing techniques and health care products and other environmental factors have affected us and our guts. These disruptors inflict harm on your health and cause you to add unnecessary weight.

- **BROAD-SPECTRUM ANTIBIOTICS**

These antibiotics have saved lives but they have also been our undoing. Each time you use these antibiotics, they eliminate the microbes in your holobiome. Even when you try to use probiotics, these microbes may not be as many as before. These antibiotics aren't only taken in drugs but they are also present in American chicken or beef. In the 1970s, when broad-spectrum antibiotics came along, the good microbes were also wiped out and the bad microbes damaged people's colon. In recent times, the use of Baytril to cure poultry against bacterial infection has had a counter-effect on humans because humans are now resistant to Cipro which is used to cure food-borne diseases.

Broad-spectrum antibiotics make you fatter because you have modified your system and then your immune system accumulates fat so your immune cells have enough to fight with.

- **NONSTEROIDAL ANTI-INFLAMMATORY DRUGS (NSAIDs)**

They are also called "gateway drugs" and they came in as a substitute to aspirin. They include Ibuprofen, Aleve, Advil and Naprosyn. They harm the barrier in your gut permitting lectins and other foreign material to enter your body. Your immune system then raises alarm by causing pain and then you take more NSAIDs to reduce pain. It is an endless brutal cycle. NSAIDs are dangerous to your mucosal barrier.

- **STOMACH-ACID BLOCKERS**

Drugs like Zantac, Prilosec, Nexium and Protonix reduce stomach acid but the stomach acid keeps bad bacteria out. The stomach acid also keeps bacteria in the large intestine by the acid gradient process. As food from the stomach goes down the gastrointestinal tract, alkaline fluids neutralizes the acid but it is when the food reaches the large intestine that it is totally neutralized. Gut bacteria thrive in an oxygen-free, low-acid environment. If there is no stomach acid to eliminate bad bacteria, they can multiply and take over the gut flora. Also, bacteria can get into your small intestine which will lead to leaky gut. In your small intestine, the bacteria, lectins and other foreign material can get into your circulatory system. With this, the immune system fights by causing pain and it comes with weight accumulation because your white blood cells need fat to fight.

Asides tampering with the task of the stomach acid, these acid blockers also kill the mitochondria's ability to produce energy in the body and can even harm the mitochondria in your brain by crossing the blood-brain barrier. These acid blockers are toxic to our energy-producing organelles and they give bad bacteria a safe abode to thrive. Also, stomach acid helps to digest dietary protein into amino acids but we have many people who are short of protein because they have no stomach acid to digest protein and absorb it. Other broad spectrum antibiotics you should avoid and their friendly alternatives (which you can use) are listed below:

- **Pain-reliever enemies:** Generic ibuprofen or Advil, Aleve, Naprosyn, Celebrex, Mobic and other NSAIDs.
- **Healthier Alternative:** Boswellia or white willow bark.

- **Acid reducer enemies:** Zantac, Prilosec (omeprazole), Protonix, Nexium and Omeprazole.
- **Healthier Alternative:** Rolaids are a low-sugar source of calcium carbonate. You can chew DGL wafers.

- **Sleep-Aid Enemies:** Ambien, Restoril, Lunesta and Xanax.
- **Healthier Alternative:** Schiff Melatonin Ultra or 3-6mg of time-release melatonin.

- **ARTIFICIAL SWEETENERS**

Sweeteners like sucralose, saccharin, aspartame and other non-nutritive sweeteners modify the gut flora and eliminate the good bacteria, giving room for bad bacteria. It also leads to weight gain because sugar tells your body that it is time to save for the rainy day (so your body accumulates fat). The taste buds on our tongue do not taste sugar but they taste "sweet". However, the body cannot differentiate between the sweeteners of sugar or caloric sources and calorie-free sweeteners. Then when you take the calorie-free sweeteners, it sends the pleasure signal and your body expects the calorie but when it does not come, your body asks for more sugar. It also disrupts your sugar clock because sugar is only supposed to be available for a season but when it is available every time, your body keeps gaining weight.

- **Artificial Sweetener Enemies:**
- Sucralose, Aspartame and Acesulfame K, as in NutraSweet, Saccharin such as Necta Sweet, etc.
- Sodas, Sport drinks, Protein bars containing any of the above
- Any foods containing Corn, Agave syrup and Pure cane sugar
- All processed food containing any of these sweeteners.

- **Healthy Alternatives**:
- Stevia, as in Sweet Leaf containing inulin
- Chicory root derivatives such as Just Like Sugar
- Xylitol or Erythritol, which are sugar alcohols
- Inulin, etc.

And just in case you didn't know, sweet taste begets an insulin reaction that makes you yearn for more, perpetuating a vicious cycle.

- **ENDOCRINE DISRUPTORS**

They are present in plastic, scented cosmetics, preservatives and sunscreens and they cause damage to the hormones. Exposure to these also cause obesity, diabetes, reproductive malfunction, women hormone's sensitive cancers, prostate-related issues, thyroid issues and impaired development of the brain and neuroendocrine systems. An example of the agent used as preservatives is butyl hydroxytoluene (BHT) which is used in treated food. These preservatives exist in different forms ranging from the Bisphenol A in plastic bottles to parabens in sunscreens and cosmetics.

Many processed food also contains an additive called tertbutylhydroquinonet which induces the immune system to release proteins which cause allergic reactions to milk, wheat, eggs, nuts and shellfish. The antibacterial chemicals found in personal hygiene products eliminate the good microbes in the holobiome. These agents also hamper your liver's ability to convert Vitamin D to its active form which prevents invigoration of the cells in the intestinal wall and gives access to lectins and other foreign material.

Hormone disruptors also imitate estrogen which sends a message to the brain to accumulate fat. An example is phthalates which is found in perfumed items and plastic wraps and has been linked to premature breast development. Humans consume it in grains, beef, pork, chicken and milk products. Arsenic which is an endocrine disruptor also mimics estrogen and the higher the arsenic intake of a pregnant person, the smaller her baby's boy penis becomes and the shorter his attention span.

Azodicarbonamide used for yoga mats is also used in bread and it hampers immune function and trigger asthma and allergies. There are various enemies and friendly substitutes.

- **GENETICALLY MODIFIED FOOD AND THE HERBICIDE ROUNDUP**

Herbicides inject poison into our systems and harm our GI tract which further tampers with our gut flora. They are found in meat and milk of livestock whose feed contains grains and beans.

Genetically modified organisms helped plants produce more lectins and develop resistance to herbicides but these GMO plants have lectins which are harmful to our gut. These are also fed to the livestock from which we get meat, eggs and milk. GMO foods lead to improper production of amino acids.

The herbicide called Roundup also gets into the body when it is sprayed on the crops we consume and we develop sensitivity to gluten which our good microbes had adapted to. Roundup affects the liver enzymes such that Vitamin D is altered into cholesterol that can be reused.

There are friendly homemade substitutes that can replace Roundup and Organic foods are healthy alternatives for GMO foods. Also, not all the things on a nutrition label are exactly the way they seem.

- **CONSTANT EXPOSURE TO BLUE LIGHT**

The way our bodies are wired, the blue light is linked to daylight and constant exposure to this light through the electronic gadgets (televisions, cell phones and some energy-saving light bulbs) induces our body to think we need to accumulate for the rainy day- which never comes. It is important that you limit your exposure to blue light and you can replace the bulbs in your room with blue-proof lights.

CHAPTER 5: HOW THE MODERN DIET MAKES YOU FAT (AND SICK)

Key Takeaways:

- *The Western foods like legumes and grains make your body prepare for war by storing fat; this leads to weight gain*
- *Legumes and grain foods contain WGA and lectins which is not good for your gut flora*
- *You need to change your eating habits to stabilize your weight.*
- *Low carb, high protein diets is not the solution*

Excess weight is usually linked to the wrong diet and sometimes it looks like you are slim because even though you eat a lot, the good microbes cannot breakdown compound foods and supply you the nutrients you need. There are various diseases that can hamper proper breakdown of food and nutrient absorption. Many people have issues with their weight and auto-immune diseases such as diabetes, asthma, arthritis, cancer and heart diseases are on the increase. Many people suffer from low energy even though they eat more food than their grandparents and engage in less work. Allergies are also very common and school kids even carry adrenaline shots with them.

We have pointed accusing fingers at the environment, the Western food supply and inactivity for our health problems but that is not the underlying problem. This is why some exercise and diet programs appear to work for a while but do not eventually work. When you put a stop to the battle raging your body, your weight will stabilize. When you alter your eating and other lifestyle habits, you are on the way to getting it right. Exercise does not help with weight loss but being active helps with weight maintenance. It also helps improve your balance and cardiovascular health; it also moderates your blood pressure and reduces stress amongst others.

There has been a paradigm shift in human food supply from hunt gathering to an agro-based lifestyle. Our ancestors did this because the crops could be preserved and the livestock could be reared; so that they could stay somewhere permanently. Or maybe they switched so humans could accumulate fat from available calories. Many people believe that whole grains and beans are the key to a healthy diet but farmers fattened their pigs and cows on corn. Pigs who are sleek and lean by nature and their digestive and cardiovascular systems are the same as humans. So, eating corn fattens humans.

Grains and beans leads to weight gain but the way out is to consume macadamia nuts. Grains and beans teach our genes to optimize the calories in order to reproduce and then quicken our deaths. Milk products also accumulate fat. Breast milk helps the weight gain and rapid growth of the offspring.

However, casein, a component of milk becomes the lectin beta-casomorphin which allows fat accumulation by encouraging inflammation. Don't forget that inflammation stimulates the immune cells to store fat to fight. The microbes in your intestines determine how fat or thin you are. Also, feces of healthy people were used to cure patients of colon infections.

Wheat Germ Agglutinin (WGA) often mimics insulin. This is how insulin works: Pancreas sends insulin into the bloodstream when sugar enters our bloodstream. Insulin then goes to the fat cells, muscle cells, and neurons to allow glucose in to give energy to these cells. In fat cells, insulin attaches to a port and then sends a message to the cell to convert glucose into fat and keep it. The insulin then detaches itself and no more sugar can enter the fat cell. In muscle cells, insulin sends a message to the cell to convert glucose into energy.

In neurons, they also need insulin to supply glucose. Once the insulin has provided glucose for the cells, it detaches for the next hormone. The issue with lectin imitating insulin arises when they attach themselves to the cell wall and send wrong signals or prevent the right information from coming in. In fat cells, WGA does not detach and continues to send signals to make fat from any sugar around the cell. In muscle cells, it attaches and prevents the real insulin from doing its job.

Therefore, the muscle does not get glucose but WGA pumps sugar into it. In nerve cells, WGA prevents the entrance of sugar and then the hungry brain asks for more calories. This leads to less muscle mass, famished brain and nerve cells and plenty fat. Grains and beans gave humans weight gain in the early times but it is working against us now.

Lectins causes weight gain when our body prepares for battle; our white cells store the fat so it does not reach our muscles and brain and we get hungrier. But when there is no war, the body does not need to store up calories or keep asking for more, so there is weight loss. Belly fat is a result of the war being fought in your gut and intestinal wall.

Low-carb, high protein, high fat diets have been notably successful but they also have their own limitations. Low carb diet often works but it is short-lived because you gain the lost weight when you go back to eating lectin-laced carbohydrates. Even if you do not eat them, your weight loss drags or stops at some point. It is usually high-protein diets and so it reduces the lectins associated with grains and beans.

The diet is based on the theory that the early man lived on buffalos and large animals but the early man actually lived on tubers, berries and nuts animal protein sources like fish, lizards, snails and insects. The ancestral diet was designed to just grow, reproduce and then die because living long and healthy does not optimize reproductive abilities. Low carb plan as weight loss is not because you ate low carbohydrate and more protein and fat but it was because you stayed away from lectin-containing foods. But even the low carbs you consume are not ancestral foods and they still contain amounts of lectin.

A ketogenic diet helps moderate sugar levels and relies on some fats for calories instead of going high protein (it involves burning fat for energy rather than glucose from carbohydrates). Limiting animal protein intake helps weight loss. People also lose weight on low fat, whole grain diet by eliminating fats that contain lectin and are high in omega-6 fats like soy, peanut, cottonseed, and canola because they cause inflammation; they use lectin-free whole unprocessed grains and they used organic grains which was free of Roundup. However, many people drop out of this diet because they do not eat much and the WGA in the wheat still attached themselves to their coronary arteries causing coronary-artery related diseases. However, Southern Chinese, Japanese and Korean's rice and Africa's yams, sorghum and millet do not contain WGA.

Elephants and humans have a lectin-binding sugar called Neu5Ac that promotes heart and autoimmune diseases while other mammals like chimpanzees have Neu5Gc which lectin cannot attach themselves to. Low carb diets involve eating a lot of red meat which is known to be a major stimulant of aging, cancer and atherosclerosis. We consume Neu5Gc when we eat meat from cattle, pigs and sheep and our body system mistakes our natural Neu5Ac for the Neu5Gc and our immune system attacks.

Neu5Gc also promotes cancer growth because it shields cancer cells from your immune system. So it is important you limit some animal protein. Diet that is also high in sugar and protein helps you gain weight and exposes you to many diseases and reduced life span. Once your genes grow and replace themselves in form of your offspring, they are ready to cease to exist. So it is important you change your diet.

Kitavans, a tribe in Papua New Guinea consume a lot of carbohydrates, saturated fat and low proteins but still have longer life span and better quality of life. How? The carbohydrates they consume are resistant starches such as yam, taro and plantains. Resistant starches are not broken down so your gut microbes feed on them the way they are and they grow, while converting them to fatty acids which your body needs. It helps the growth of your gut microbes which means thicker barriers to keep lectins out. It also makes you feel full longer and consume less food.

Other tribes like the Okinawans, Cretans and Sardinians also live long disease-free lives because they also consume foods that promote the growth of gut microbes. They also eat less protein and get calories from other sources. The change in food trends have led to more obese kids in recent times. Pizza and chicken are high on the list with their lectin-based ingredients which pumps estrogen and weight gain into children. The changes in food supply, personal care products, lighting have led to your health issues but it is time to turn things around for your health.

PART II: INTRODUCING THE PLANT PARADOX PROGRAM

CHAPTER 6: REVAMP YOUR HABITS

Key Takeaways:

- *There are four rules on the Plant Paradox Program you have to stick to*
- *There are three phases on the program*
- *You do not have any excuse not to stick to the program if indeed you want to stay healthy*

You have to stick to four rules to regain good health and it all boils down to taking care of your gut.

- The first rule is that what you stop eating has more effect than you what you start eating.

- The second rule is to treat your gut microbes properly and they will take care of you in return. Stop feeding the bad bacteria what they thrive on; yes, excommunicate the sugar, refined carbs and junk food.

- Third thing, you need to erase the idea that fruit is health food. The message fruits send to your brain is to accumulate fat and the fructose in fruits is harmful to your kidneys. The only fruits you can eat are green papaws, green bananas, green mangoes and ripe avocados because they contain resistant starches which are good for the gut microbes.

- The fourth rule is that you are what the thing you eat ate. So if you are eating industrially raised livestock, you are what they feed them: corn and soybeans.

Your gut microbes feed on a lot of the calories you consume and they make little clones which power special fats for you. As you heal your gut and your lectin tolerance grows, your food supply will widen. Just watch your animal protein consumption. Most of the fast food you consume is made from corn and this corn has lectin injected into it. Once you eat the burgers or drink cow's milk, you are mostly consuming corn.

Genetically modified corn also causes brittle bones in chicken and when you consume the chicken, you are loading yourself with lectin. Products from livestock are also usually loaded with aflatoxins and other toxic by-products from fungi which are harmful to humans and animals and usually lead to cancer and genetic changes. So be careful with animal protein.

You and your gut microbes are supposed to have a beneficial relationship but you often feed the bad bugs more and they take over your body. What to do is to starve the bad microbes and feed the good ones so they would help you restore your body. They also help you crave the good things your body needs to stay healthy. The Plant Paradox program supports the right animal fats. The program helps you stay healthy by drawing a diet that grows your good microbes. The program is in three stages:

- **Stage 1:** A three-day cleanse fixes your gut, strengthens the good microbes and starves the bad ones. This will stabilize your gut flora but you must move to the next phase as fast as possible to make sure the bad microbes do not make a comeback.

- **Stage 2:** You have to stop some foods and start eating some. Do this for two weeks and you would be used to it in 6 weeks. You would have to stop consuming lectin, GMO foods, crops treated with herbicides and saturated fats.

  You can't do this without avoiding sugar in all its forms, industrial livestock and their by-products, and every hormone disruptor products.

  Reduce your omega 6 fats to the barest minimum. You can take nuts, guacamole or half an avocado. Instead, your diet should consist of leafy greens, tubers and food that contain resistant starch.

  Eat more of omega-3 fats from avocado, fish oil, macadamia nuts, etc.

Do not eat more than 8 ounces of animal protein from fish, shellfish and poultry fed with omega-3. Limit dairy products except from breeds of cows that make Casein A-2.

- **Stage 3:** Cut down consumption of animal protein not less than 2 ounces and not more than 4 ounces.

For those who have issues giving up their usual sources of protein, cooking your beans with pressure cooker destroys the lectins and can prolong your life and even boost your memory. Vegetarians can eat little amounts of correctly prepared legumes. On the other hand, the lectins in oats, rye and wheat cannot be destroyed so avoid them totally. You may want to check out a pressure cooker.

The right amount of protein gives your body energy and helps you build muscle but most people take in more protein than they need. Overconsumption and breaking down of these proteins is linked to higher blood sugar levels, obesity and a reduced life span. You only need 0.37 grams of protein per kilogram of body weight. So you can do the calculations. Do not eat more than a single 3 ounce serving per day. This is also because we recycle the protein we already have.

There are some excuses you may give before you go ahead with the program. The first is that you are already slim, fit and active. You may be outwardly active and physically active but you may have an internal health issue. The second is that you may be thinking that the program needs a deep understanding of human metabolism and nutritional concepts. All you just need to know is the food to avoid and the one you need to eat. The third excuse is that you are too old or it is too late to alter your eating habits. However, your age does not matter once you are willing to feed your gut microbes and advance your health. You really do not have an excuse not to move on with the Plant Paradox program.

CHAPTER 7: PHASE 1: KICK-START WITH A THREE-DAY CLEANSE

Key Takeaways:

- *The first phase has three components*
- *It is to immediately move to the next phase to prevent a vengeance of the bad microbes*

You need to sanitize your gut flora before you begin to "sow the seeds" of good health. The cleanse will chase the bad microbes in your gut and will make it faster to achieve your desired result. It's just like weeding out the bad plants and tilling the soil for cultivation. This cleanse consists of three elements.

Element 1: On and off the Menu

- Do not eat dairy, grains, fruit, sugar, eggs, soy, corn, canola or other oils and livestock by-products.

- On your menu should be vegetables and little intake of fish or pastured chicken. Vegetables like cabbage, broccoli, Brussels sprouts, cauliflower, kale, lettuce, mustard greens, celery, radishes, parsley, onions and seaweed.

- The protein you should eat should not be more than 8 ounces of salmon, shellfish or pastured chicken in a day.

- The fats and oils should be from avocado, olives, coconut oil, macadamia oil, sesame seed oil and you can have guacamole or the right nuts as snacks.
- You can have a "green" smoothie in the morning, 8 cups a day of mineral water or tap water and green, black or herbal tea.
- You can sweeten your tea with Sugar Leaf.
- Sleep and exercise well too.
- Your veggies have to be organic, the fish and shellfish should be self-caught and the chicken should be pastured.
- Use avocado oils, low heat for olive oil and no heat at all for hempseed and flaxseed oils.

Element 2: Prepare the "soil" and remove the "weeds"

- Use herbal laxatives to cleanse your gut. Swiss Kriss is an example of a good herbal laxative
- Other things you can use to banish the bad microbe include peppermint oil, strawberry leaves, calendula flower, hibiscus, peach leaves, etc.

Element 3: Getting help from Supplements

You can use natural supplements to end the reign of the bad microbes. They are not very mandatory except you suffer from leaky gut or autoimmune issues. Supplements like grapefruit seed extract, mushroom extracts, Oregon grape root extract, and black pepper work wonders.

After this fast, it is important that you move to the next stage so as not to re-invite the bad guys and contaminate your gut flora. With the cleanse, you would have lost some pounds, changed the balance of your gut microbes, reduced inflammation and be ready to move on to the next stage.

During the cleanse, your body will crave all those unhealthy foods but you have to stick to the fast.

CHAPTER 8: PHASE 2: REPAIR AND RESTORE

Key Takeaways:

- *There are foods you have to eat and there are foods you must not eat*
- *Feed your good microbes and make sure the bad ones are famished*

Delaying health issues and not putting an end to it is not a very reasonable solution. Your body can cure itself once you stop eating the foods that hamper it from healing. The first step to begin the six week repairing process is to rid yourself of all the lectin-laced foods that cause holes in your intestinal wall. You can go back to chapter 6 to remind yourself of the rules. The goal is to malnourish the bad microbes by not eating the foods they live on. This will help to hasten your healing.

In your attempt to eat the right foods, your body may protest and you may have headaches, low energy and muscle cramps. However, you have to strive to stick to the list (eat the "Yes please" foods and avoid the "No" meals). The program is a forever eating habit and not some quick fix.

The Say "Yes please" involves oils like algae oil, coconut oil, macadamia oil, red palm oil, sesame oil, perilla oil, walnut oil and flavoured cod liver oil.

The acceptable nuts are walnuts, pistachios, coconut, coconut milk, tiger nuts, hazelnuts and chest nuts.

Acceptable energy bars include cinnamon and acceptable sweeteners are Stevia's SweetLeaf and Just Like Sugar.

Six ounces of Red Wine per day is acceptable.

Vegetables like broccoli, Brussels sprout, carrots, artichokes, asparagus, mushrooms and cauliflower are acceptable.

Foods like slim pasta, wild-caught fish, cabbages, collards, chicory, lobster, 1 ounce of cheese or 4 ounces of yoghourt, sardines, oysters, anchovies, kimchi, onions, and chives are acceptable.

Dairy products such as goat yoghourt, goat milk, goat cheese butter, coconut yoghourt, sheep cheese, casein A-2 as milk creamer, French/Italian and Switzerland cheese and organic heavy cream are also on the Say "Yes please" list.

Avocados, blueberries, blackberries, strawberries, cherries, pomegranates, kiwis, apples, peaches, figs, apricots, plums, dates are the acceptable fruits. Eat green plantains, green mangoes, green bananas, yams, sorghum, millet, cassava, persimmon, celery root, tiger nut and parsnips in moderation.

Eat pastured poultry, resistant starches (special kinds of tortillas, bread, bagels, coconut flakes and cereal) and meat from venison, elk, boar and bison.

The just Say "No" list includes:

-   Refined starchy foods like pasta, rice, potatoes, milk, bread, tortillas, pastry, flour, crackers

- Sweeteners like Saccharin, Aspartame, and Acesulfame K
- Vegetables like brown rice, peas, legumes, tofu,
- Beans of any kind
- Frozen yoghourt, Ice cream, cheese
- Fruits like cucumbers, zucchini, pumpkins, eggplants, melons, tomatoes, bell peppers
- Oils from soy, grapeseed, cottonseed, corn, sunflower, vegetable and canola.

The foods you would be eating on the program are beneficial to you and your gut microbes. The lectins in the food on the program have been interacting with humans for humans of years and so your body can handle them. You just have to filter the lectins that enter your body. People have frequently to make bread, rice and pasta white because it is the WGA that makes them brown so "whole grain goodness" is a hoax.

Beans have high lectin content. Undercooked and canned beans are disasters waiting to happen. Also stay away from unfermented soy products too. Dairy products are also harmful because they contain casein except the ones from sheep and goats but all of them have Neu5Gc. The lectin contained in chia seeds make them more harmful than the omega-3 fat they give. Another source of lectin is peanuts and cashew nuts which are legumes, not nuts. Corn and Quinoa grain are also heavy suppliers of lectin which harms our intestinal wall.

Eggplants, potatoes, tomatoes and peppers also contain lectin but the Italians and Indians often find ways to get rid of the lectin. However, Americans do not. Fermentation or pressure cooking helps to get rid of the lectin in legumes and nightshades but it does not work like that with grains. The squash family including pumpkins and zucchinis help you accumulate fat and lectin. Many plant lectins also hide in animal proteins; it is important to control your animal protein intake. You should also limit your oils that come from seeds that have lectin like canola oil and coconut oil; use Perilla oil.

Minimize your intake of cream and cheese too. The Perilla oil contains omega 3 fatty acid which is friendlier for your heart and keeps your gut wall intact. You can also use the other oils on the acceptable food list. Saturated fats increase your hunger and food intake but fish oils help you moderate your food consumption.

Stick to the food list to enable you to totally eliminate the bad microbes. The cleanse curbs them but some still hang around to exploit your carelessness. Avoid what is on the "No" list to starve the bad bacteria and feed your gut microbes the foods on the "Yes" list to grow them.

If you have leaky gut, avoid cabbages before you include them into your acceptable list. Your gut microbes need sugar that you cannot digest and they can thrive on to perform. They are called prebiotics like the fructooligosaccharides and it helps the gut microbes produce more mucus. Do not use acid blockers or NSAIDs because they may frustrate your efforts at maintaining your gut flora. Consume fish oil and increase your level of vitamin D to repair your intestinal wall and rebuild stomach acid with grapefruit seed extract and betaine.

You can have Quest bars or the Human Food bars for animal protein, green smoothie, muffins and plain coconut milk yoghourt for breakfast; guacamole and sliced jicama as an afternoon snack, salad and olive oil for lunch and fish, salad and acceptable pasta or noodles for dinner. You can also have resistant starches for dinner, your gut microbes would be glad you did! If after six weeks you still have difficulties, you can still take your time on this phase or even live a healthy life on this routine.

On the other hand, if you experience weight loss, pain relief, autoimmune problems clears, let's keep moving.

CHAPTER 9: REAP THE REWARDS

Key Takeaways:

- *You can test your lectin tolerance at this stage*
- *You have to limit your intake of animal protein*
- *Pressure cook beans to get rid of lectin*

At this stage, you have begun to reap the fruits of your labor: a beneficial relationship between you and your gut microbes which breeds quality health, weight control and long life. If you are following the rules, you would see an improvement in your weight and you would no longer experience pain caused by your autoimmune issues. It is a lifestyle diet, not a one-time business. You would know if your gut flora has been repaired and if your gut microbes would continue to sustain you and you can check if you can start eating foods with some lectins (only after you have spent 6 weeks in the second stage). If you are not in a rush to test your lectin tolerance, you can keep eating the meals in stage 2.

You can use some quick tests to know if you can consume small amounts of lectin.

- Have your bowel movements returned to normal?
- Is your poop well formed?
- Have your joints stopped aching?
- Has your skin cleared?
- Is your face now smooth?
- Do you now sleep all through the night without any inconvenience?
- Is your energy level high?

- If you were overweight, have you reduced?
- If you were underweight, have you filled out?

It is only if your answers to the questions are yes that you can leave stage 2. If you also have autoimmune diseases, just keep avoiding the foods in the "No" list for now.

There are some cultures that seemingly have varied diets and stay healthy but there is a common thread which is that they limit their intake of animal protein. You can try to play safe by spacing time between meals or limiting protein intake and overall calories for some days, weeks or even months. Stage 3 is really a lifestyle not like stage 1 (which is 3 days) and stage 2 (minimum of 6 weeks) which have lengths. This phase would help you to live long without health problems. You can begin to introduce small amounts of lectin depending on your lectin tolerance.

Keep eating the foods on the Say "Yes please" list. When you gut has been healed, consume more ketogenic fats which your microbes do not store as fat but uses to power you. Stay away from the foods on the Say "No" list and if you can, you can try cucumbers or zucchini. If you can handle them, try seeded peppers and heirloom tomatoes (give space of a week to see if you handle them). You can then try pressure-cooked legumes and grains except rye, oats and wheat (which contain gluten). Eat less frequent meals to give your body time to rest after the digestion process. Limit your animal protein and let your source of protein be from certain vegetables, mushrooms, nuts and hemp. You can also stick to the natural supplements suggested in stage 2. Don't disrupt your circadian rhythm; get 8 hours of sleep and exercise well. Avoid the blue light too.

Beans also have resistant starches and are good as long as you get rid of lectins (which you can by using a pressure cooking). The safe grain is the Indian white basmati rice but if you have diabetes or you want to lose weight, avoid it. You can still take sorghum and millet. You can also try to start eating some members of the nightshade family like tomatoes, peppers and eggplant in limited quantities and they must be peeled and deseeded. Do the same with squash. Stay away from foods that cause weight gain or make you consume a lot. Eating meat makes you gain weight and red meat contains Neu5Gc which has been linked to cancer. You can stick to fish or shellfish.

The Blue Zones are parts of the world where people have longevity and these areas include the Italian area of Sardinia, Okinawa in Japan, Loma Linda in California, the Nicoya Peninsula of Costa Rica and the Greek island of Ikaria. In their diet, they restrict animal protein. However, the Mediterranean consume grain which contains lectin which attaches to their cartilage. Though they counter the lectins by eating certain vegetables, olive oil and the red wine, they still have some autoimmune diseases.

Research has shown that cutting down on animal intake aids long life. The lower your IGF-1 (insulin growth), the longer you live and the less susceptible you are to cancer. And eating less sugar and less animal protein gives you lower IGF-1. It is better to derive your protein from plant source and maybe add a little fish.

When you fast, your body burns ketones for energy so you can stay without glucose for a while. If you are not ready to let go of animal proteins, an alternative is to stay away from animal proteins for just five days in a month. A five-day fast from animal proteins can give the same results. Another substitute is to cut calories twice a week and then eat typically for the rest of the week. A third choice is to space your mealtimes (about 16 hours) to develop your metabolic flexibility. All these work to have improved health.

For those who have very serious health issues, there is an intensive care on the program called the Keto Plant Paradox Intensive Care Program which will be discussed in the next chapter.

CHAPTER 10: THE KETO PLANT PARADOX INTENSIVE CARE PROGRAM

Key Takeaways:

- *Your body prefers ketones to glucose*
- *The program is for those who have health issues because their mitochondria is overworked*
- *Fruits are not good for your kidneys*

People that have serious health problems all have a common cause: lectins wreaking havoc in the gut. For example, in Parkinson's disease, white blood cells called glial cells protect neurons and when they discover lectins, they defend these neurons so much that the neurons do not get nourishment and they die. Too many lectins also affect how mitochondria convert sugars and fats.

Mitochondria generate an energy molecule called Adenosine Triphosphate (ATP) and they often divide themselves. However, there is a limit to what they can do at a time and they need a little period to rest. Up until now, mitochondria worked during the day, converting sugars and fat and then burn your ketones as fat at night because they are not breaking down sugar or protein. The mitochondria often slow down their work at night.

Before now, they worked a lot during summer because there was surplus food and then even stored fat in your belly. It was not an issue because during winter when there was not a lot of food, they could use the fat they stored to make Adenosine Triphosphate. But the problem arises when you consume so many calories and the mitochondria cannot handle all of it, they become tired and do not work. At this point, all the calories that come in cannot be converted and are stored as fat in your belly. Also, your brain does not receive energy and starts crying for more food.

Mitochondria cannot handle overconsumption and then insulin sends a message to the fat cells who then convert the sugar into fat which leads to weight gain. If you now add the saturated fats and lectins, it is not a surprise your mitochondria have gone on leave.

Sadly, you cannot just start cutting down your sugar and protein and make life easier for your mitochondria, and then all is well. This is because if you have high insulin, the hormone-sensitive lipase will not convert fat into ketones. This is the reason low carb, high protein followers often stop at some point. The high protein in the diet converts into sugar which releases insulin and stops your body from converting fat into ketones. This leads to low energy supply and exhibits as headaches and low carb flu.

You have to reduce sugar and proteins to drop your insulin levels and save your mitochondria the stress. Dropping your insulin means unblocking the ketones that can give you energy. There are plant fats that have ketones and can help you in ketone production. Coconut oil, red palm oil, goat butter and ghee are great sources of ketones. Don't think you can eat your cake and have it by eating these good fats and still consuming a huge amount of animal protein. You would only be playing yourself because you will never be able to convert fat into ketones while consuming animal protein.

The mitochondria in cancer cells cannot use ketones to generate energy unlike normal cells. In its place, they thrive on sugar fermentation used by yeasts and bacteria and they would rather ferment sugar in fructose not glucose. So it is important to not feed the cancer cells.

Also, diabetic patients do not need insulin to pass ketones into your body. Fat and ketones should be your buddies and you should avoid protein, carbohydrates and fruits like a plague. This is because diabetes is caused by too much protein, sugar and fruit stressing your mitochondria. Fructose is an underlying cause for kidney failure, and high blood pressure. With this intensive care program, you would stop consuming the things that terrorize your kidneys like lectins, fruits and huge amounts of animal protein.

The program saves your kidneys. Health issues arise from mitochondria meltdown and instead of the basic plant paradox program, the intensive care program further restricts animal proteins and totally banishes fruits and seeded veggies. The program also sticks to the Say "Yes" list and Say "No" list on the basic program but with strict restrictions on animal proteins and huge frowns on fruits (except those listed as resistant starches) and seeded vegetables.

There are a few specifics:

- The only acceptable fruits are avocados, green bananas and plantains, green mangoes and green papayas
- Stick to macadamias as nuts
- The only acceptable dessert is frozen sugar free coconut milk. Goat ice-cream should not even be near you
- Eat chocolate only if it is 90% cacao
- Avoid animal proteins altogether if you have cancer
- Eat egg yolks
- Good sources of fat are walnuts and hemp seeds and use olive oil and perilla oil

Spacing out time between meals would also help in the program because your mitochondria would have time to rest.

During the fast, you can take a spoon of coconut oil or an Adapt bar so you would not be feeling weak.

For cancer, memory and neurological patients, it is better you take your time on the program. People with obesity, diabetes or kidney failure can switch to the basic plant paradox programs if you have achieved some level of progress after three months. The goal is not to rush through the program but to have a healthy lifestyle.

CHAPTER 11: PLANT PARADOX SUPPLEMENT RECOMMENDATIONS

Key Takeaways:

- *There are important supplements you need to take to further boost the effect of the program*
- *Do not take these supplements and still eat the Western foods*

Taking supplements is a critical component of the Plant Paradox program. The reason the program is called "Plant Paradox" is because plants are like our frenemies. They are our curse and our blessing. You cannot get all the nutrients without taking supplements.

You need vitamin D3 supplements; use 5000 IUs daily and 10000 if you are an autoimmune patient. You also need Vitamin B especially Methylfolate and Methylcobalamin (B12) to help lower your cholesterol. Take between 1000 to 5000 mcg tablet of B12 and 1000 mcg of methylfolate.

There is also a list of these supplements known as G6, namely:

Prebiotics: These are the compounds your gut microbes thrive on. It helps them grow and function properly. They include psyllium husks, breast milk which contains galactooligosaccharides, inulin. A teaspoon of inulin powder and psyllium husks each and a packet of galactooligosaccharides would do.

Polyphenols: They are beneficial when they are broken down by your gut microbes. They also stretch your blood vessels. Sources of polyphenols include grape seed extract, pine tree bark extract and polyphenol in red wine. Take 100 mg of grape seed extract and 25 to 100 mg of pine tree bark extract. Others include green tea extract, berberine, cocoa powder, cinnamon, mulberry and pomegranate.

Lectin blockers: There are a few lectin-absorbing products that disallow lectin from reaching your gut wall. They include products like GundryMD Lectin Shield, Osteo Bi-flex. These products contain D-mannose (the active ingredient in cranberries).

Green plant phytochemicals: Your gut microbes love greens so greens reduce your cravings for the things the bad microbes thrive on. A good source of this is spinach which reduces your hunger for simple sugars and fats; another good source is modified citrus pectin. Modified citrus pectin reduces kidney stress by starving the bad microbes.

Long-chain Omega-3s: Many people are deficient in brain-boosting fats and a great source of this is egg yolks, fish oil, sardines and anchovies. Those who have sufficient omega 3 fats have a better memory and bigger brain than those who are short on omega 3 fats.

Sugar Defense: The product is GundryMD Glucose Defense which combines chromium, zinc, selenium, cinnamon bark extract, berberine, turmeric extract and black pepper extract. You can use two capsules in a day to help your body control the sugars you consume. You could also use CinSulin which combines chromium and cinnamon. You can mix this with 30mg of zinc, 150mcg of selenium, 250mg of berberine twice a day and 200mg of turmeric extract twice a day.

If you are following the intensive keto program, you may experience leg cramping because of your strict compliance to the diet. However, you can use supplement potassium magnesium aspartate to end the cramping. You cannot use the supplements while sticking to the regular Western foods and expect perfect health. The supplements are only used as augmentations of the plant paradox program and not alternatives to the program. The supplements only work when your eating habits are in tandem with the plant paradox program.

Made in the USA
Lexington, KY
20 September 2018